Dot Markers
Activity Book
Sea Animals

(Guided Big Dots)

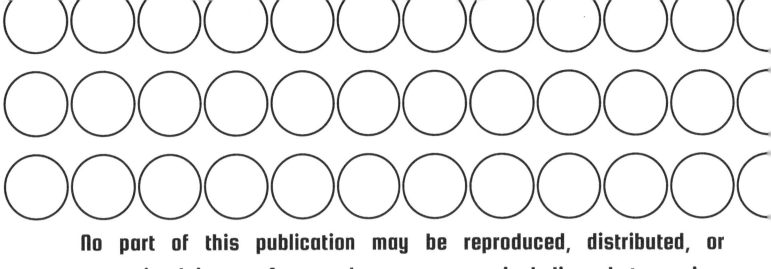

Artworks from Freepik.com & Creativefabrica.com or licensed for commercial use.

For Further Communication:
Email: azulancreatives@gmail.com
Facebook: fb.com/azulancreatives
Website: www.azulancreatives.com

Test Your Colors Here

Let's Color The Sea Animals!!!

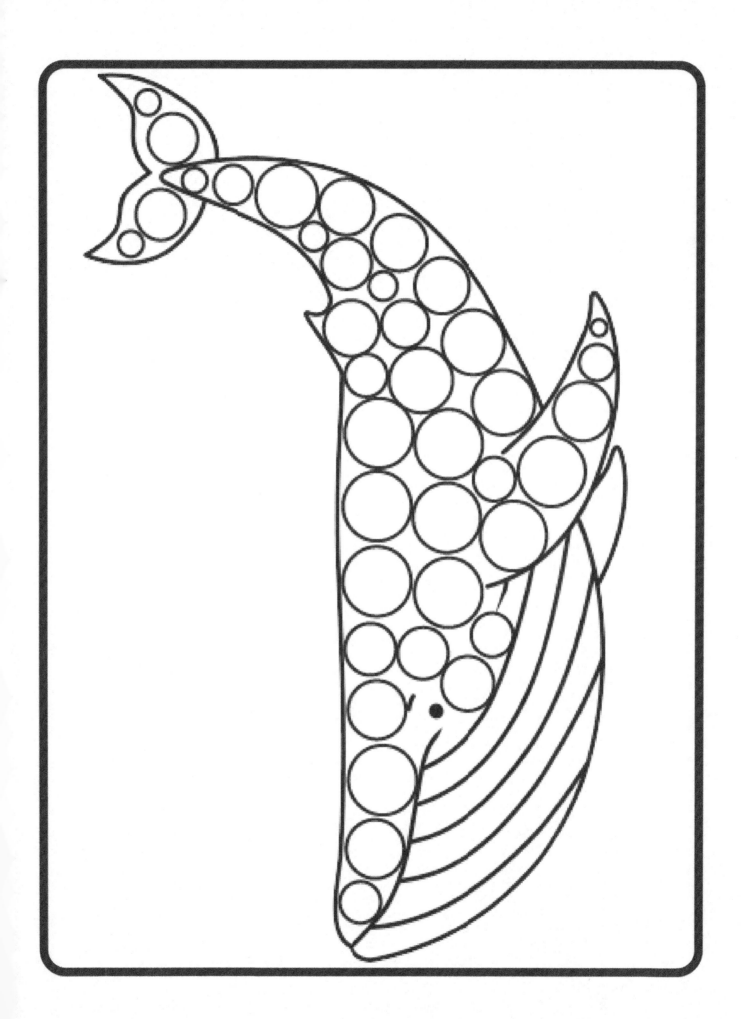

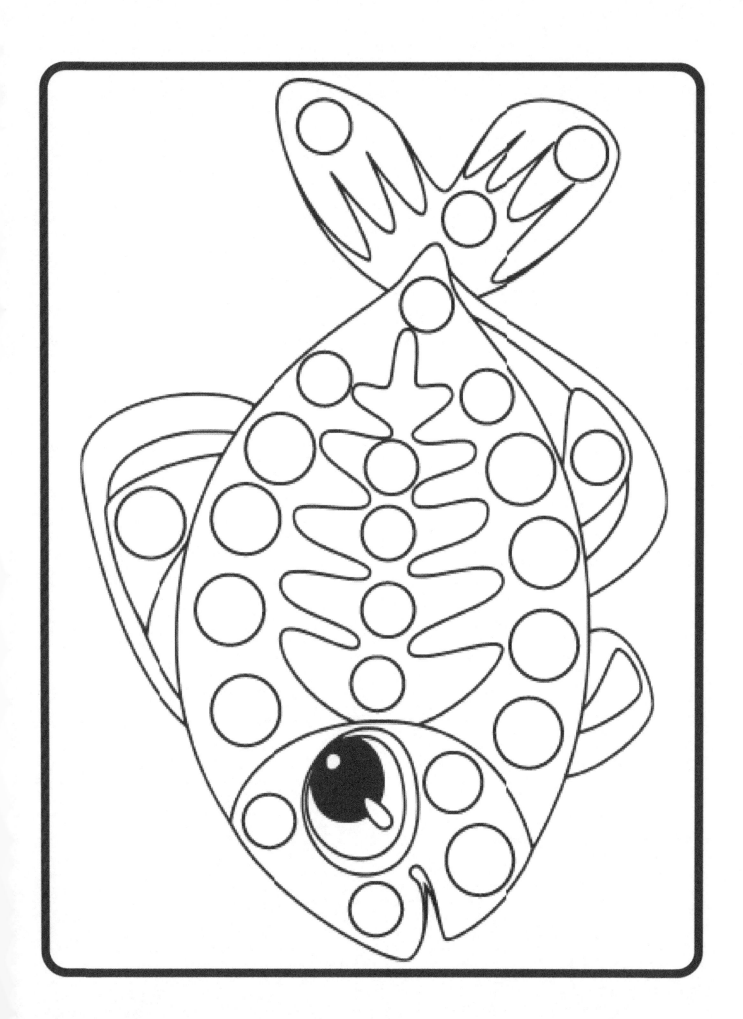

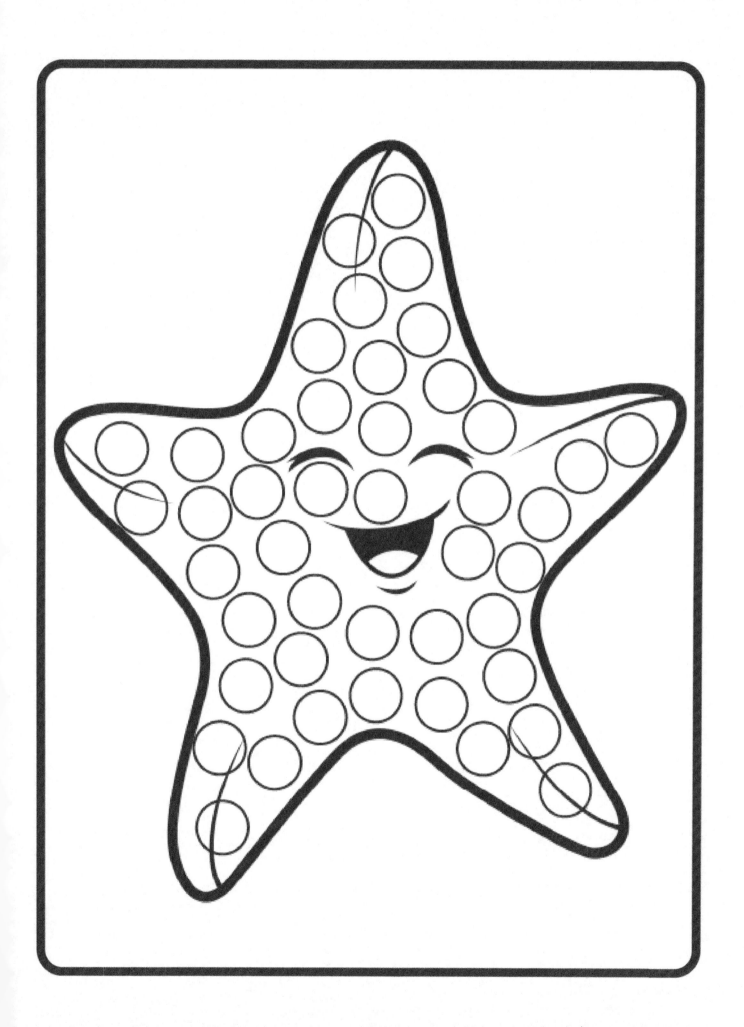

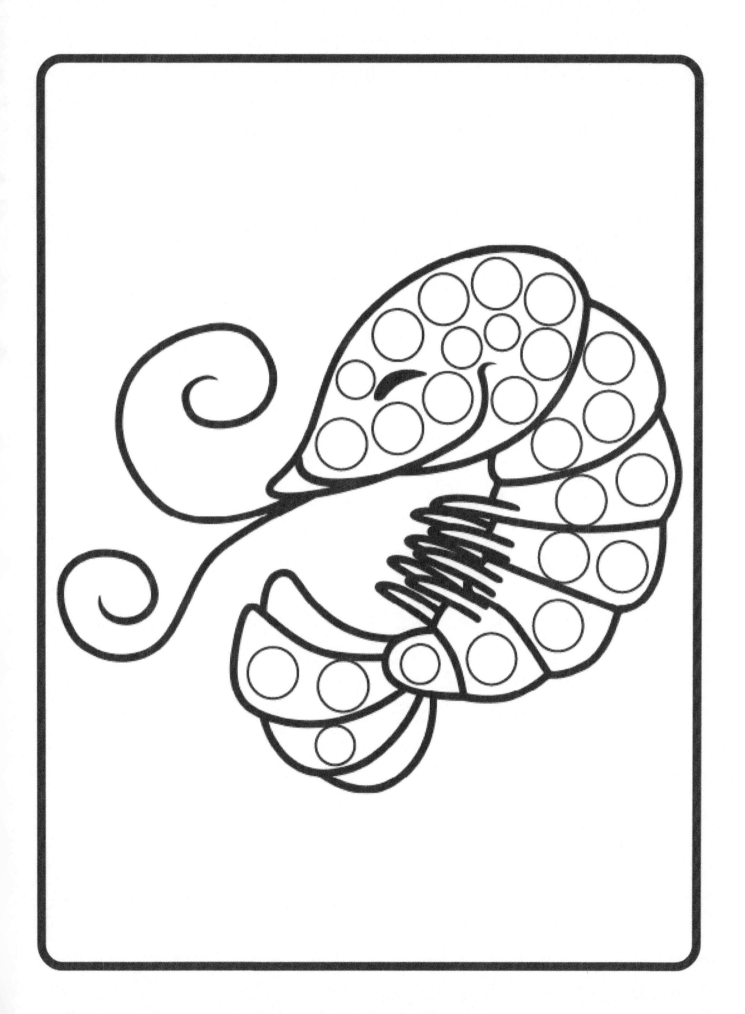

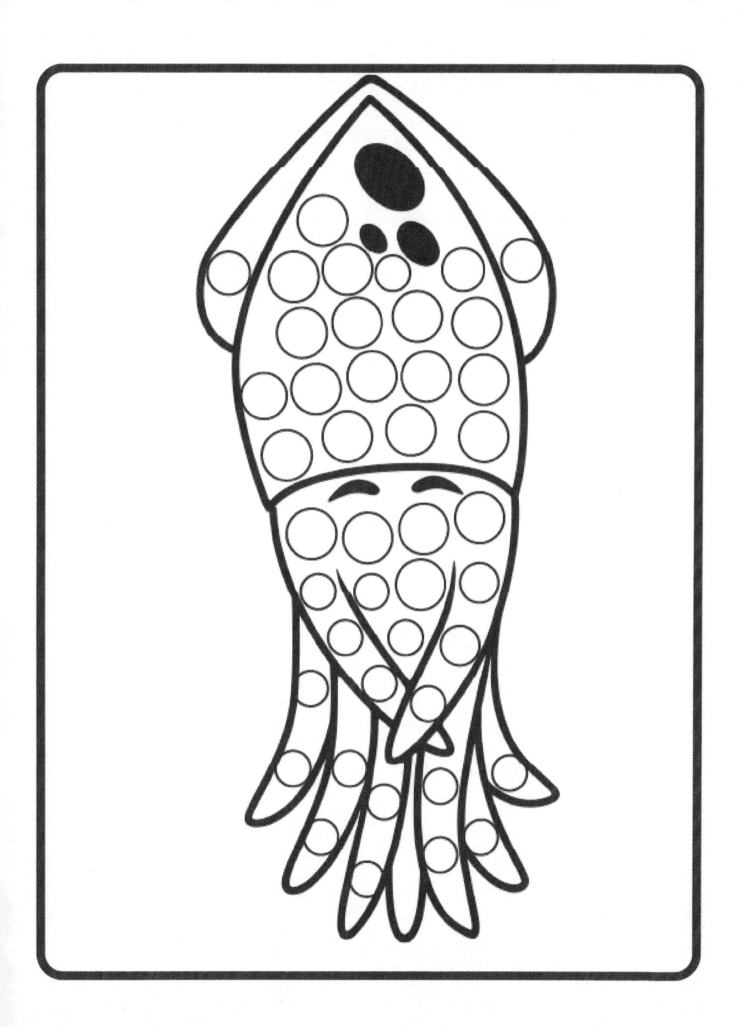

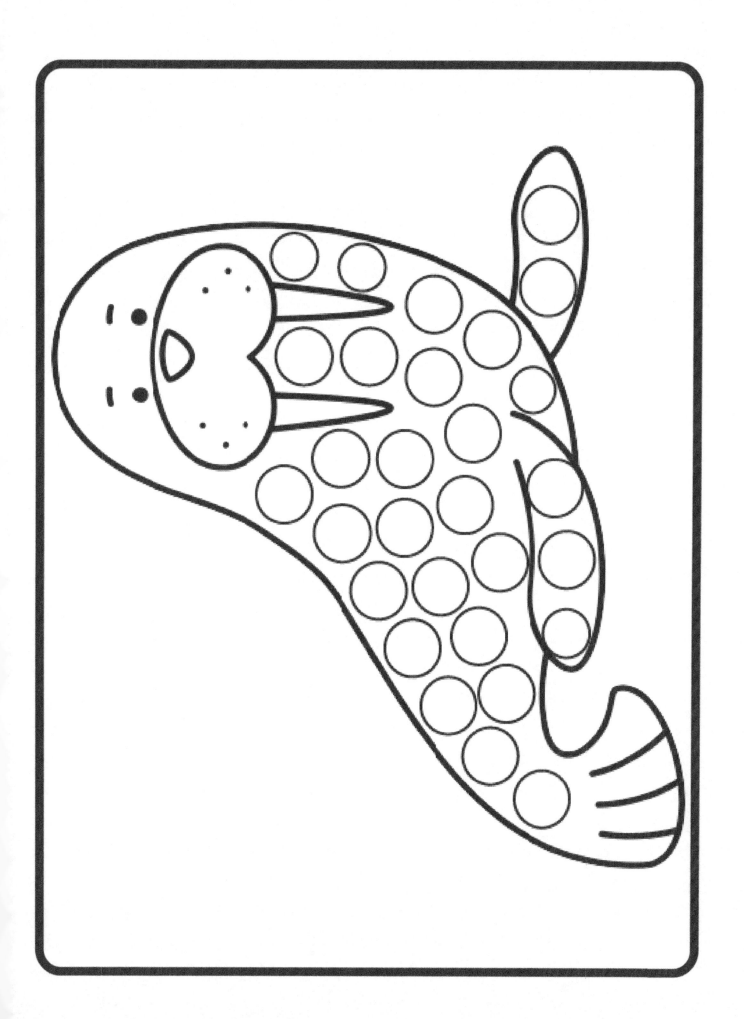

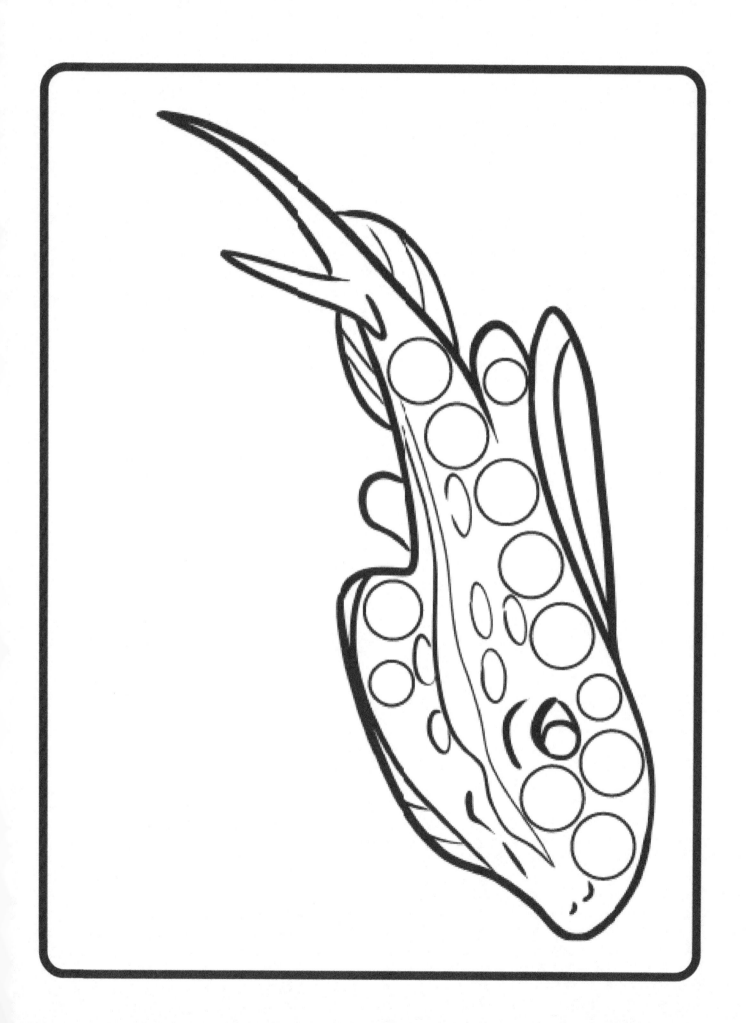

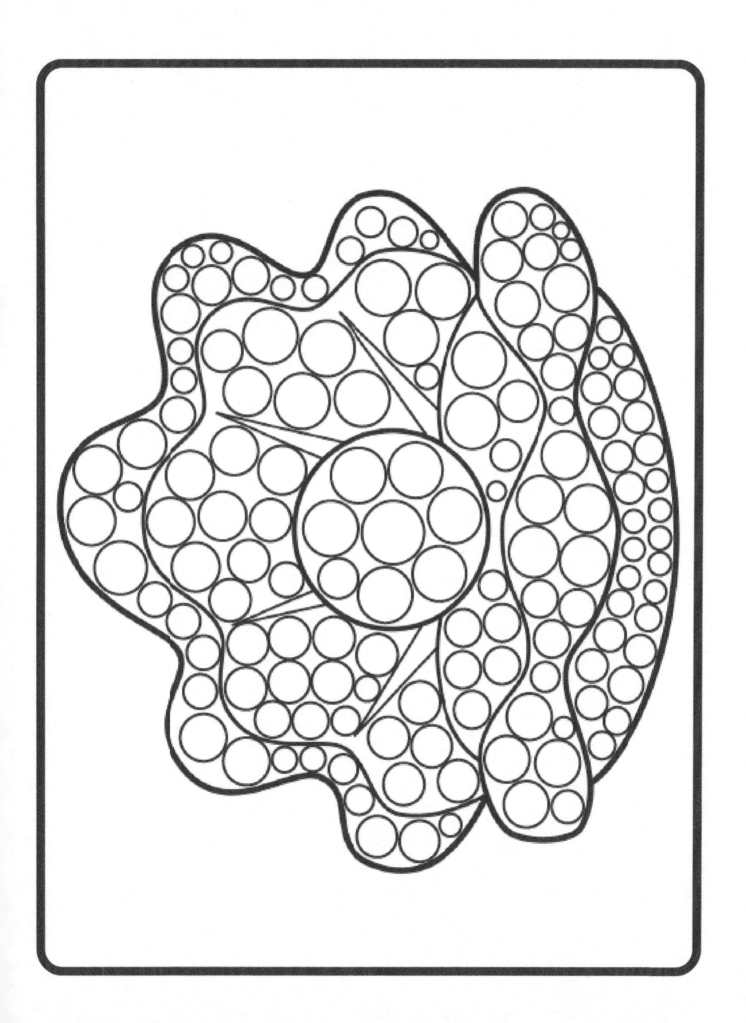

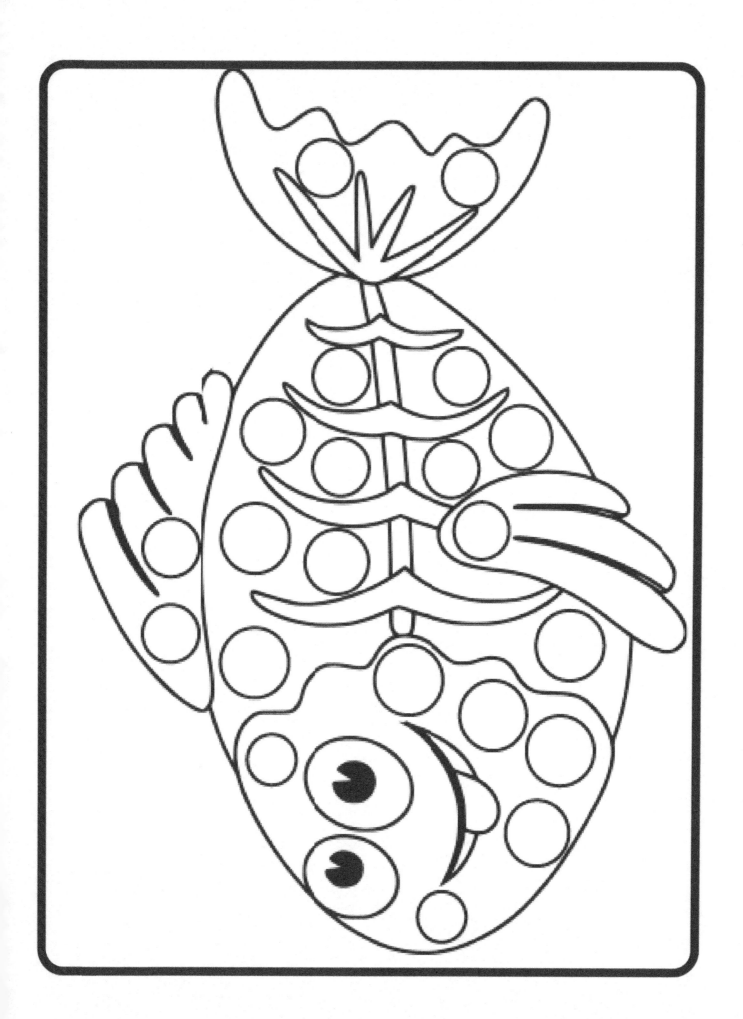

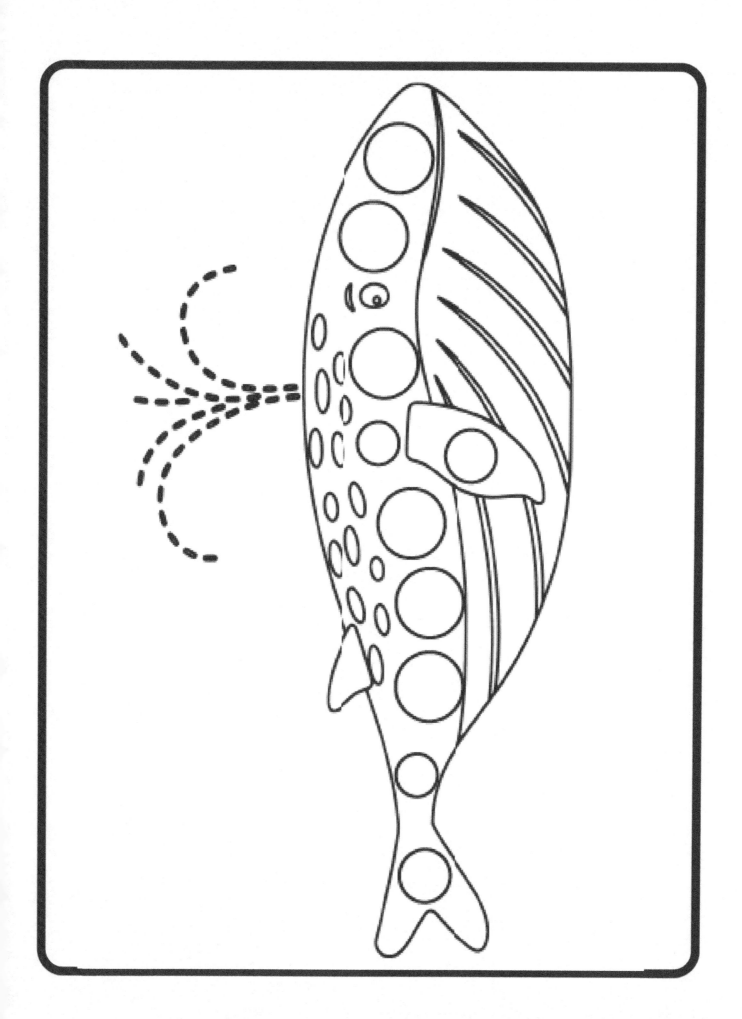

Made in the USA
Monee, IL
27 October 2023

45307182R00050